OUR SACRAMENTS

INSTRUCTIONS IN STORY FORM FOR USE IN THE
PRIMARY GRADES WITH COLORED DRAWINGS
ACCOMPANYING TEXT ACCORDING TO MODERN
EDUCATIONAL METHODS

BY

REV. WILLIAM R. KELLY

Author of "Our First Communion" and "The Mass for Children"

2018

ST. AUGUSTINE ACADEMY PRESS
HOMER GLEN, ILLINOIS

Nihil Obstat

ARTHUR J. SCANDAN, S.T.D.
Censor Librorum

Imprimatur

✠ PATRICK CARDINAL HAYES,
Archbishop of New York

NEW YORK, March 1, 1927

This book was originally published in 1927
by Benziger Brothers.

This facsimile edition reprinted in 2018
by St. Augustine Academy Press.

ISBN: 978-1-64051-068-5

March 4, 1927.

Dear Father Kelly:—

I am more than pleased at your latest contribution to the illustrative literature in which you have been so exceptionally successful. "Our Sacraments," I am sure, will prove a very helpful adjunct to the catechism in concentrating the children's minds on the traditional answers of the more formal method of teaching.

With a blessing on yourself, the teachers and pupils who will use this very attractive and instructive book, I am,

Faithfully yours in Christ,

☩ Patrick Card. Hayes

Archbishop of New York.

MY DEAR BOYS AND GIRLS:

WHEN Our Lord was here on earth He helped people to understand His teachings by telling them stories.

Now in this little book there are stories that will help *you*.

They will help you to understand what the Church teaches about the seven wonderful sacraments.

As you read the stories and look at the pictures, you will see for yourselves what the sacraments are and what they do, and your catechism lessons will, I hope, be made easier and more interesting.

Father Kelly

Feast of the Ascension, 1927.

OUR SACRAMENTS

SACRED SIGNS

(THE SACRAMENTS)

Tom and Ann and their Uncle John were watching a big army airplane which had come down on the fields near their home.

Something had happened to the tank. Little by little the gasoline had dripped out until the plane was forced to descend.

The mechanic made the necessary repairs; a new supply of gasoline was put into the tank, and, after some delay, the airplane was ready to be off again.

With a great roar the propeller began to go around; and, as gracefully as a bird, the huge plane left the ground, sailed up into the blue sky and soon disappeared.

"It's almost like going to heaven," said Ann.

"Yes, isn't it," her uncle agreed; "and did you notice that the airplane could not go up until gasoline was put into the tank?"

"The gasoline gives it power," said Tom, in a knowing way.

"It's the same with our souls," Uncle John declared. "Unless they get power from God, they can never go up to heaven.

"That power for our souls is called the 'grace of God'. Grace gives us power to do good, to fight evil, and to go to heaven."

"How do we get grace?" asked Ann.

"It's a gift of God," replied Uncle John.

"Every time we pray, God gives it to us. But it is through the sacraments especially that He gives us His grace. You remember, don't you, what the catechism says about a sacrament? It is an outward sign made by Our Lord to give grace. And you know how many sacraments there are?"

"Yes," answered Ann. "There are seven sacraments: Baptism, Penance, Holy Eucharist, Confirmation, Matrimony, Holy Orders, and Extreme Unction."

"Good girl," said her uncle. "But did you ever see anyone receiving the sacraments?"

Tom spoke before his sister could answer. "Surely," he said; "both of us have made our first Confession and received First Communion."

"Well, then, you have seen two of the sacraments. Of course, you don't remember having been baptized, but you were, and that makes three sacraments you have received. When the baby is baptized next Sunday, you will see for yourselves what Baptism is like. And next year, with God's help, you will see me ordained a priest. What sacrament shall I receive then?"

"You will receive Holy Orders," Ann said.

Then she asked: "Do you think mother will take us to see you ordained?"

"Don't worry; I'll tell mother and **father** I'm going to save front seats for you."

Tom and his sister were delighted.

"When will it be?" they asked.

"Next June," replied their uncle; and the very thought made him smile. "But I'm sure," he added, "that I'll miss my fine vacations on this farm."

"Won't you come again when you are a priest?" asked Tom.

"Yes, but only for a few days; after that, I must go away to the missions."

Later in the afternoon, while walking through the village, they passed a shop over which a large shoe was hanging.

"Why is that shoe there?" Uncle John asked.

"It's a shoemaker," cried Tom.

"You mean," said Uncle John, "it shows that a shoemaker is inside."

A few moments later, they passed a pole

striped like a peppermint stick. Uncle John turned to Ann. "What is that for?"

"It shows people there is a barber shop inside," she replied.

"Well, children," explained their uncle, "if there were no signs on the stores, strangers would not know what was going on inside. But, as soon as they see the signs on the outside, they can easily understand what is going on inside.

"People need signs," he added; "they can't get along without them. That is one reason why Our Lord gave us the seven sacraments. The sacraments are sacred signs; each one of them gives grace. By means of these outward signs, God lets us know we are receiving inward grace.

"Think again of that airplane," said

Uncle John. "It was made to go up, but without power it could not go up.

"So it is with our souls. They are made to go up to God, but without power they cannot do so.

"We cannot get power for our souls from gasoline, can we?"

The children laughed.

"Well, then, where shall we get it?"

"From the sacraments," cried Tom and Ann together.

"And what are the sacraments, Tom?" asked Uncle John again.

Without waiting a moment, Tom answered, "The sacraments are outward signs instituted by Christ to give grace."

CLEANSING WATER

(BAPTISM)

The bell in the tower was striking four o'clock as the godfather and godmother came into church with the new baby. Uncle John led the way to the baptistry, a little room separated from the church. In a few moments the parish priest entered and greeted the family pleasantly. Then he put on his linen surplice and a stole.

"Before we begin," he said, "I am going to ask the godmother to open the baby's dress at the neck. In a little while, I shall have to mark a cross with holy oil on the baby's chest and back."

The godparents then stood where they were told, and the ceremony began. Tom and his sister remained at one side of the

baptistry with their uncle. How interested they looked!

"What name is the baby to have?" asked the priest.

"Matthew," said the baby's father.

Turning to the infant, the priest said, "Matthew, what do you ask of the Church of God?"

Now, Matthew was sound asleep. The

godparents answered for him. They said, "Faith."

"What does faith bring you to?" And the godparents replied, "Life everlasting."

Of course, babies cannot answer any questions; that is why the godparents are present. They speak for the baby, and they know it is their duty to watch over their godchild, and to see that he is brought up a good Catholic.

A few moments after the priest had begun to read the prayers, the children saw him reach over to a small box on the table. From it he took a pinch of something which he put on the baby's tongue.

"What is that?" Ann whispered.

"Salt," said Uncle John. "You know, salt is used to preserve meat and other foods. Well, the priest is praying that this *blessed* salt may preserve the baby's soul and keep it good forever."

The priest then made the sign of the cross with oil on the baby's chest and back.

"That is blessed oil," said Uncle John.

"People use certain kinds of oil to give light and strength and comfort. They put oil into lamps and it gives light. Runners have their muscles rubbed with a special oil

before they race, and their muscles are made strong. And, as you know, olive oil is used to bring comfort to the sick.

"By using *blessed* oil, the Church tries to make us see that the soul is now receiving light and strength and comfort."

The priest went on reading the prayers, and then stopped to ask three questions:

"Do you renounce Satan?"

The godparents replied, "I do renounce him."

"And all his works?"

"I do renounce them."

"And all his pomps?"

"I do renounce them."

"Oh, Uncle, what does 'renounce Satan' mean?" asked Ann.

"It means, 'Do you turn your back on the devil?'

"The godparents make a promise for the baby that he will turn his back on the devil and on all the devil's works."

Next the children heard the priest ask: "Matthew, wilt thou be baptized?"

And the godparents answered for him, "I will."

"Watch carefully now," said Uncle John, "the priest is going to baptize the baby."

The godmother stepped up to the font and held the baby's head over it. The godfather stood at her side and placed his hand on the infant as the priest told him to do.

Then the priest dipped a small shell into the font, filled it with baptismal water and poured the water over the child's head.

While pouring the water, he said the following words carefully and clearly:

"I baptize thee in the name of the Father and of the Son and of the Holy Ghost."

"Ah," said Uncle John in a low voice, "now the baby's soul is as clean and white as snow. Original sin is all washed off."

"Original sin?" asked Tom. "Isn't that the sin for which Adam and Eve were punished?"

"Yes," said Uncle John, "the stain of that sin is on the soul of everyone who comes into the world. As a special favor to His Mother, Our Lord did not let that stain come upon her soul for a single moment. And, of course, sin could not touch the soul of Jesus. It is true, He let St. John baptize Him in the River Jordan, but that baptism was not given to wash away original sin.

It was simply to show the Jews how much He honored St. John the Baptist.

"So, except for Our Lord and Our Lady, original sin has stained everybody's soul."

"Is that stain on me?" asked Tom.

"Original sin was on your soul until you were baptized; then it was washed away. And it was on the baby's soul until this moment. But now the stain of sin is gone, and his soul is filled with grace."

"I learned in school that Baptism is a sacrament which cleanses us from original sin," said Ann.

"That is right," replied Uncle John, "but don't leave out the rest of the answer. Doesn't Baptism make us Christians and children of God?"

"Yes," smiled Ann, "and it makes us heirs of heaven."

"Ah, now you have it all," said her uncle. "Baptism is a sacrament which cleanses us from original sin, makes us Christians, children of God and heirs of heaven."

"Matthew is a Christian now. That

means he belongs to the Church of Christ.

"And he is a child of God, for God has adopted him and made him a member of His family. All the saints in God's family will now look on him as a relative. They will help him to get to heaven for now he has a right to call heaven his home.

"St. Matthew will take good care of him, I'm sure. The saint whose name we bear always watches over us in a special way. That is why we give saints' names to children.

"See the white cloth which the priest is placing on Matthew," said Uncle John. "It is a sign to show how white and clean the baby's soul is now."

A moment later, the priest handed the godparents a lighted candle, and the children heard him say: "Receive this burning

light; keep your Baptism without blame; keep the Commandments of God, so that when Our Lord comes again, you may meet Him, together with all the saints in heaven, and live forever and ever."

The priest gave little Matthew a special blessing; the godmother wrapped him up in his robe; and the family started for home.

On the way, Uncle John told the children

how necessary it is to be baptized.

"Our Lord made the apostles understand that no one can go to heaven without being baptized," he said.

"That is why the Church lets anyone baptize when there is danger of death. If no grown person is near, even a child can baptize by pouring ordinary water over the person's head, and saying, 'I baptize thee in the name of the Father and of the Son and of the Holy Ghost.'

"Well, children," said Uncle John, as they came in sight of the farmhouse, "now you know much more about the sacred sign of Baptism. You saw the priest pour the water over the baby, and you heard him say the holy words of Baptism. Of course, you could not see the baby's soul, nor could you see what was happening there."

"Oh, but the sign showed us what was happening inside," cried Tom.

"Yes," said his uncle, "it showed you that sin went out and grace came in."

That evening there was a happy party. A number of relatives and friends had come to see little Matthew; they rejoiced with the family because a new soul had been washed in the cleansing water of Baptism and made an heir of heaven.

THE MERCIFUL FATHER

(PENANCE)

Six fat pigs looked up eagerly as they heard familiar voices. Uncle John and the children threw into the pen armfuls of corn husks. It was not a pretty sight to see the greedy animals devouring their food.

"This puts me in mind of a story," said Uncle John. "Let's sit away over there under that shady tree, and I'll tell it to you."

"Is the story about pigs?" asked Tom.

"Not exactly," said his uncle, "but the pigs reminded me of it."

"Oh, tell us all about it," begged the children.

"Just a moment, just a moment; before I begin, I want to ask a few questions,"

Uncle John said. "They will help the story."

"Who can tell me the name of the sacrament in which our sins are forgiven?"

"Confession," shouted Tom.

"Penance, the sacrament of Penance," cried Ann.

"Ann's answer is better," said Uncle John, with a smile. "We call it the sacrament of Penance; confession is one part of the sacrament.

"You must be sorry for all your sins and promise God not to sin again. That's the first part of the sacrament. The catechism calls that part 'contrition'.

"Then, you must tell your sins—that part is 'confession'.

"Next, the priest takes away your sins —that part is called 'absolution'.

"Lastly, you must say or do the penance,

which the priest tells you—that part is called 'satisfaction," because we try to satisfy God by our prayers and good works.

"So, there are four parts to the sacrament of Penance." Uncle John counted them on his fingers:

"Contrition, confession, absolution and satisfaction.

"Which part do you think is the most important?" he asked.

"I think confession is," said Tom.

"Oh, no," replied Ann; "absolution counts most because it takes away the sins."

"Well," said their uncle, "every part counts, of course, but the most important is contrition, for if we are not really and truly sorry for our sins, all the rest is useless. That is why we are told to kneel down and pray for sorrow before going into the confession box.

"Having true contrition means that we are sorry, not for ourselves, but because we have offended God."

Uncle John picked up an apple.

"If a greedy boy were to eat too many of these and make a little pig of himself, that would be a sin.

"If, then, he were sorry just because he became sick, would that be true sorrow for his sin?"

"No, it would not," said Ann. "He would be sorry just for himself."

"I know a boy who was caught stealing," said Tom. "He was sorry because his father punished him. That wasn't true sorrow, was it, Uncle?"

"No, it was not; he should be sorry

because he offended God by his stealing."

Uncle John stood up and threw the green apple. His aim was good. It went right into the pig-pen. Tom tried to do the same.

"Too far for me," he said, as Ann laughed at his attempt.

"Now I'll tell you that story that the pigs reminded me of," said Uncle John, as they sat down again. "It explains all the different parts of the sacrament of Penance.

"Long ago there lived two brothers who had a rich father," he began. "The younger brother was very jolly. He was always whistling and singing. Everybody liked him.

"But the other brother was mean and stingy. It is true, he did what his father wanted, but he was such a faultfinder, and was so unpleasant, that people kept away from him.

"Now, when they grew up, the jolly lad made up his mind to go far away.

"He told his father he was going to leave, and asked for his share of the family fortune. It was a shame for him to leave his old father like that, wasn't it? But, you see, he was thinking only of himself and his own pleasure. So, off he went.

"After a time, the young man found that his money was all gone. Money does not last long when it is thrown away for foolish and sinful things.

"The miserable fellow was alone in a strange country. His companions, who had helped to spend his money, now laughed at him. About this time, there came a famine; food became very scarce. The young man began to starve.

"Finally, when he was weak with hunger, a farmer hired him to take care of pigs. And the only food he could get was the stuff given to him for those animals!

"Ugh!" said Ann and Tom. "Did he die?"

"No. While sitting by the pig-pen one day, thinking of his old father, he suddenly made up his mind to go home.

" 'Perhaps my father will let me return as one of his hired servants,' he thought.

"Every day the old father used to gaze down into the valley, hoping that his boy might come back. He had almost come to believe that the lad had died, when one morning he saw him climbing the hill.

"He ran down the slope to meet him. What a welcome he gave the poor, ragged wanderer! With arms about each other, they went up to the house.

"Now, what do you think the other brother did? He refused to join in the welcome. He was actually angry to see his brother come back at all.

"But the good father put a gold ring on the young son's finger, gave him fine, new clothes, and called in the neighbors for a great party.

"Our Lord Himself told that story," said Uncle John. "He wanted to show us that He will always forgive if only we come back to Him and tell Him how sorry we are for our wrongdoing.

"The kind-hearted father is like God, who welcomes back every sinner; and the brother who would not forgive, is like many mean persons who have no pity for sinners."

Across the fields came the welcome sound of a bell.

"Dinner!" shouted Tom and Ann.

As they started for the farmhouse, Uncle John said: "Do you see, children, how that story shows us the four parts of the sacrament of Penance?

"The young man had contrition, because he was really sorry for having offended his father; he confessed when he told his father how sorry he was; he received forgiveness; and then by the good life he led after that, he tried to make satisfaction.

"I know some other stories about Penance," continued Uncle John. "Perhaps I'll tell them later on."

"Yes! Yes!" cried Tom and Ann together. "It's too hot to play today. Let's go back under that shady tree after dinner to hear the rest."

"Good idea!" agreed their uncle. "We'll do that."

After the meal, Uncle John kept his promise.

"This is the coolest spot I know of," he said, as they sat down under the tree. "Now, what was I saying when we left off?"

Tom spoke up: "You were telling us about the father who forgave his son."

"Oh, yes!" said Uncle John, "Our Lord told that story to comfort poor sinners. He was very kind to sinners when He was here on earth.

"One day a paralyzed man, who could not walk a step, lay before Him. The crowd watched to see what Jesus might do. Our Lord knew the man needed help for his soul even more than for his body. So He simply said to him:

" 'Thy sins are forgiven.'

"Evil people in the crowd laughed.

" 'How do we know his sins are taken away?' they asked. They wanted to see if Jesus would cure the man's body.

" 'Which is easier,' asked Our Lord, 'to take away sins, or to say: Arise, take up your bed and walk?'

"Then He added: 'That you may know I have power over sin, I will cure this man.' And He did.

"Our Lord gave His priests power to forgive sins. Just before He went up to heaven, He said to His first priests, the apostles:

" 'Receive the Holy Ghost. Whose sins you shall forgive, they are forgiven them; whose sins you shall retain, they are retained.'

"Ever since then," said Uncle John, "priests have been forgiving sins.

"Sometimes, however, a priest isn't within reach when a person is most anxious to have his sins forgiven."

Uncle John was silent for a moment.

"I remember an accident that happened one day when I was in the city. A poor fellow was struck by an automobile. I was the first to go to him.

" 'Get me a priest,' he groaned. He was terribly injured. Somebody offered to rush for a priest. Meanwhile, I bent over and said the Act of Contrition for the dying man.

"He kissed the cross of my rosary. All he could say was: 'My Jesus, mercy!'

"Before the priest or the ambulance could get there, he died.

"I feel that Our Lord forgave that man his sins," said Uncle John, "for the Church tells us that, at such times, if we say only the name of Jesus, and have real love for Him in our hearts, we shall be forgiven.

"Of course, we all hope to have the priest with us when we die. But if we should be in danger of death, and the priest cannot get to us in time, we should make an act of perfect contrition.

"And God, who is a merciful Father, will forgive us as the kind old father in the story forgave his son."

"Uncle John," said Tom, "when will you be able to hear confessions?"

"After I'm made a priest, next June," smiled Uncle John.

"Will you be able to understand the people in the foreign missions?"

"Some of them speak English," answered his uncle, "especially the boys and girls who have gone to the mission schools. And, then, the priests learn the language of the people after a short while.

"I was talking to an old mission priest not long ago," Uncle John went on to say. "He was telling me how interested the mission children are in their First Confession."

"Do they have confession boxes in those places?" Ann asked.

"Yes, they go to confession just as Catholics do everywhere.

"They begin by saying: 'Bless me, Father, for I have sinned.' They let the priest know how long it has been since their last confession; then they tell their sins.

"You know the rest, Tom," said Uncle.

"Yes!" Tom replied. "After they have confessed their sins, the priest tells them to say certain prayers as a penance. They recite the Act of Contrition and the priest takes away their sins. Last of all, they do not leave the confession box until the priest says, 'God bless you.' "

Uncle John clapped his hands. "Good! You could teach the pagans yourself."

"I hope I shall, some day," said Tom.

"Well, then, Mr. Teacher, if you were speaking about the sacrament of Penance, could you show there is an outward sign which gives grace?"

Tom could not answer. "You tell us, Uncle," he said.

"You have seen the priest make the sign of the cross; and you have heard him say the words of forgiveness, haven't you?" Uncle John asked.

"Yes," replied Tom. "He does that after we have told our sins."

"At that moment your sins are taken away and you receive God's grace," continued Uncle John; "that is, if you have done your part. The priest's part and your part together make the outward sign of this sacrament. Your part is to be truly sorry, to confess your sins right, and to be ready to do your penance."

"Is it a sin if you don't say your penance?" Ann asked.

"Yes, Ann," her uncle replied; "that is, if you mean to skip it. It is best to say the penance immediately after confession. Then you can be sure you have done your duty to God."

At that moment father came up.

"The agents in the city called a few minutes ago. Can you go down with me, Uncle John?"

"Surely," he answered, rising at once. "Sorry, children; we'll have to stop now."

"Uncle John is interesting, isn't he?" said Ann, after her uncle had gone.

"Right you are," replied Tom. "I hope I'll be able to remember what he told us. Some day I may be telling those stories to other boys and girls."

BREAD FROM HEAVEN

(HOLY EUCHARIST)

"Well," said Tom's father, as he climbed into the motor-boat, "this is a good day's work, isn't it?"

Uncle John smiled.

"You and Tom are pretty good fishermen," he agreed.

The family had gone down the river on a fishing trip and picnic. Uncle John had had poor luck: one fish was his only reward, while Tom and his father had caught eight.

The sun was setting as the boat started for home.

"Supper time," said mother, opening one of the baskets.

"Sure enough!" shouted Tom, with delight. "I had almost forgotten about my supper."

Everybody laughed.

"You remind me," said Uncle John, "of those people in the Gospel story. You were so interested in everything all afternoon, that you never gave a thought to eating.

"It makes me think of the time that a big crowd followed Our Lord all day long."

On and on they followed Him, until many of them were far from home. They had brought nothing to eat, but simply could not turn back. And no wonder!

"Never had they heard anyone speak as Our Lord did. Never had they seen anyone do the things He did. One after another, the sick, blind, crippled and the deaf and dumb had come to Him. And He cured them all.

"As the hour grew late and dusk came on, the apostles became anxious. They wished Our Lord would send the crowd away. But Jesus knew that many had to go a long journey. Perhaps, too, He could hear little children crying with hunger.

"He asked one of the apostles where bread might be bought. The apostle shook his head. There were no stores in that place. Even if there were, the apostles could not buy food for such a number.

"Just then another apostle came to Our Lord. 'There is a boy here,' he said, 'who has five barley loaves and two fishes. But what are these among so many?'

"Now, what do you suppose Our Lord did? He ordered the crowd to sit down. Then, blessing the bread and the fishes, He told the apostles to give this food to the people. And as fast as they gave away the bread, more bread appeared in the baskets; as fast as they handed out the fishes, more fishes appeared in the baskets.

"The people were astonished. But they ate and ate until they were filled.

"Then Our Lord said to the disciples:

" 'Gather up the fragments that remain, lest they be lost.'

"And the disciples filled twelve baskets with the bread and fishes that had been left over.

"So overjoyed were the people that they rose up shouting that Jesus should be their king. Our Lord had to flee to the mountain to escape them."

"Did the people go home after the meal was over?" asked Tom.

"I suppose a few did," replied his uncle, "but most of the crowd stayed and the next day they sought Our Lord again.

"When He saw the crowd He scolded them a little. He wished so much to speak to them about food for their souls—but they were thinking of food for their bodies.

" 'You seek Me,' said Our Lord, 'not because you have seen miracles, but because you did eat of the loaves and were filled.'

"Then He promised to give them a wonderful bread. He meant, of course, Holy Communion. But they, still thinking of ordinary bread, said to Him:

" 'Lord, give us always this bread.'

"Our Lord answered: 'I am the living bread which came down from heaven. If any man eat of this bread, he shall live forever. The bread which I shall give is My flesh for the life of the world.'

"One year later," said Uncle John, "Our Lord kept the promise He had made. The apostles were gathered with Him at the Last Supper, the night before He died.

"Then it was that Our Lord took bread into His sacred hands. With His eyes lifted up to heaven, He blessed it, broke it, and gave it to His apostles saying:

" 'This is My Body.' "

"And in the same manner He took wine and changed it into His Precious Blood.

"The promise was kept. At that moment Our Lord gave us the sacrament of the Holy Eucharist. He gave Himself to be the food of our souls.

"At that moment, too, He made His apostles priests, and gave them, and all priests after them, power to change bread and wine into His Body and Blood.

"So today," continued Uncle John, "millions of God's people love the Holy Eucharist, and delight to receive that wonderful bread.

"Great numbers of people come from every part of the world to attend a Eucharistic Congress. These are usually held every few years, in a different city, with beautiful ceremonies. In this way the people show

the world their special devotion to Jesus in the Holy Eucharist.

"Here," said Uncle John, "is a picture of the great crowd at the Eucharistic Congress in Chicago."

"But tell me, Tom," he asked, "do you know what the Holy Eucharist is?"

"The Holy Eucharist is the sacrament
which contains the Body and Blood, soul

and divinity of Our Lord Jesus Christ, under the appearance of bread and wine," answered Uncle John.

"But," added Ann, "why is it called Eucharist at one time, and Holy Communion at other times?"

"Oh, the name of the sacrament is the Holy Eucharist," said her uncle. "When we receive the sacrament, it is called Holy Communion. Don't you remember, the catechism says:

" 'Holy Communion is the receiving of the Body and Blood of Our Lord'?

"Another name you should know is 'Viaticum.' When the priest carries the Holy Eucharist to the dying it is called 'Viaticum.' That word means 'a companion for the journey.' Therefore, when we receive Viaticum, we have Our Lord with us as a

companion on the journey to heaven.

"The Holy Eucharist is also called the Most Blessed Sacrament because no other sacrament is so holy as this."

"How do you know which name to use?" asked Tom.

"Just think of this," said Uncle John; "the name of the sacrament is the Holy Eucharist. When you receive the Holy

Eucharist, it is called Holy Communion. When the priest gives Holy Communion to the dying, it is called Viaticum. And when you genuflect in church, it is to the Blessed Sacrament that you give honor.

"A light burns before the altar to remind us that the Blessed Sacrament is there.

"As the star over Bethlehem told the Wise Men that Jesus was there, so this light tells us that Our Lord is present in the Most Blessed Sacrament.

"The Wise Men knelt at the crib. Was it only a Babe that they saw? Ah, no; they believed in Him and adored Him as God.

"We come to the altar rail to receive Holy Communion. Is it only bread that we see? Ah, no; we believe it is Jesus, the same good Jesus before whom the Wise Men knelt."

"Wouldn't it be fine if we could see Our Lord sometimes, as He used to be on earth!" said Tom.

"Our Lord did appear to some people in that way," Uncle John replied. "There is a story about a pagan officer who was watching Catholic soldiers receiving Holy Communion long ago.

"He was amazed to see a beautiful Infant in the Holy Communion. As some of the soldiers received, he saw the Child smile with joy. But from two or three men the Infant turned in sorrow.

"After the Mass, this pagan hurried to tell the priest what he had seen. It did not take long for the priest to show him how great a favor he had been granted. With his own eyes he had seen the Infant Jesus.

"Shortly afterwards he was baptized and became a great Catholic ruler. You may read about him some day. His name was Widukind, Duke of an ancient German tribe called the Saxons.

"Widukind had fought bitterly against the Christians for many years. He hated Christ. But after he had seen Our Lord in the Blessed Sacrament, he could not do enough for Him."

"I suppose he went to Communion very often after that," said Ann.

"Yes," answered her uncle, "and what a different man he became. No longer did he lead an evil life. Instead of fighting against Christ, he fought for Him like a Christian soldier."

"I wonder," said Tom, "why the Infant turned away and cried when He saw those soldiers."

"Because they were not fit to receive Him," replied Uncle John. "They must have had mortal sins on their souls. To receive Holy Communion in such a way is a sacrilege. A sacrilege is one of the greatest sins."

"They should have made a good Confession before they went to the altar," Ann said.

"Does God forgive people like that?" asked Tom.

"Yes, He does," Uncle John answered. "Even those people can be forgiven if they are sorry, and tell in confession what they have done."

*   *   *

The little motor-boat rode on through the moonlit waters. Lights shone out here and there from the houses along the shore. Except for the clang of a cow-bell, or the bark of a dog, the silence was not broken.

When at last the boat reached the village, the children were fast asleep. They were a tired little pair as they climbed the hill to the farmhouse. But both agreed that the day was one of the best they had ever spent.

CHRIST'S SOLDIER

(CONFIRMATION)

The people of the village were all excited. A regiment of soldiers had come in on a special train. With flags flying and bands playing, a thousand men in uniform were marching from the station to their summer training camp.

Uncle John was there to greet them, and to welcome his old friend, Father Daniel, the army chaplain.

Tom and Ann were delighted when the chaplain invited them to visit the camp with their uncle.

At dinner that day they could speak of nothing but soldiers. How they watched Uncle John as he spoke of the battles which Father Daniel's regiment had fought in France!

In their mind's eye, they could see the priest crawling over the ground to help the wounded and dying, while bullets and shells whistled all around him.

"He was a real soldier of Christ," said Uncle John. Think of how much good he and other priests did during the war.

"They said Mass for the soldiers, also heard their Confessions, gave them Holy

Communion and prepared them for death. When the regiment was away from danger they preached to the soldiers, gave them instructions, and helped to make recreation time pleasant. At all times they tried to keep the men thinking of God.

"Many saints of the Catholic Church have been soldiers. One of the most famous was St. Martin of Tours."

The children clapped their hands. "Tell us about him!" they cried.

"After dinner," said Uncle John. He folded his napkin and went out to the veranda. Ann hurried to clear the table and get the dishes washed. When the task was finished, she sat down and waited eagerly for the story.

"The father of St. Martin was a pagan and an officer in the Roman army," Uncle

John began. "He hoped his boy would some day become a general. When Martin was about sixteen years old, he was placed in the cavalry."

"Pardon me, Uncle," said Ann; "what is the cavalry?"

"It is that part of the army that rides on horseback," her uncle answered.

"Well, in the army," he continued,

"there were some Christian soldiers. Martin talked with them about Our Lord. Even as a small boy, he had wished to become a Christian. But his pagan parents would not let him.

"Martin and some soldiers were riding out of the city one day when they met an old beggar. He was half naked and shivering as he stood in the snow.

" 'Help me! Help me!' begged the old man.

"The soldiers just laughed at him. But good-hearted Martin could not pass him by like that.

"He took off his splendid soldier's cape and, with one blow of his sword, cut it in two. Then he gave half to the freezing beggar.

"As they rode on, the soldiers made fun

of Martin, who had only half a cape to cover his shoulders. But in their hearts they must have admired him.

"That night Martin saw a vision. Before him stood Our Lord. And around Our Lord's shoulders was the half cape that Martin had given the beggar.

"Turning to the angels who were with Him, Jesus said: 'Martin has covered Me

with this cloak.' What a wonderful reward to have Our Lord come and thank him for the gift!

"Soon after the vision, Martin was baptized. When he finished his service in the army, he made up his mind to become a priest.

"Years later, he became a famous missionary, and then was made bishop of the city of Tours in France. God gave him great power. He worked so many miracles that to this day he is called the 'wonder-worker of Tours.'

"You see, then," said Uncle John, "that Martin left the army to become a soldier of Christ. He preferred to fight for Our Lord. We, too, must take part in the fight against the devil and against evil in order to save our souls.

"Our Lord knew that this fight would be hard without His help, so He gave us the sacrament of Confirmation to make us strong and brave.

"Ann, do you remember what Confirmation is?"

"Yes," she replied. "Confirmation is a sacrament through which we receive the Holy Ghost to make us strong and perfect Christians and soldiers of Jesus Christ."

"Correct," said Uncle John.

"We should never forget that we are soldiers of Jesus Christ. When the devil tempts us, we must fight against him like good soldiers. And if evil persons try to get us to do wrong, we must fight against them also. We have nothing to fear, because the Holy Ghost is with us. He will stay with us until the very end of our lives in order to help us win the victory.

"Do you know how the Holy Ghost helped the apostles?" asked Uncle John.

"No," answered Tom. "Won't you tell us?"

"Well," said Uncle John, "the apostles were very much afraid after Our Lord had been put to death. They feared that they might be killed too; but since Our Lord had commanded them to stay in Jerusalem and wait for the Holy Ghost to come, they obeyed Him.

"For ten days they prayed and waited in the upper room of a house in Jerusalem.

"Suddenly, on the tenth day, there came a sound from heaven like a mighty wind. It filled the whole house where they were sitting. Upon the head of each apostle there rested a wonderful light. The apos-

tles were all filled with the Holy Ghost.

"They began to speak in different languages. When they went into the street, crowds gathered as they saw St. Peter start to speak. Many strangers from far-off lands were there. How astonished they were!

"Persons from more than eighteen countries heard St. Peter as if he were speaking their own languages. All wondered, saying one to another, 'What does this mean?'

" 'We do not know this man's language, yet we can understand him. Truly this must be the work of God; it must be a miracle!'

"Before night had come, three thousand persons were converted and baptized.

"The enemies of Our Lord arrested the apostles. They put them into jail and beat them. 'Stop this preaching about Christ,' they said, 'or we will put you to death.'

"But when the apostles were let out of jail, they preached all the more. No longer were they afraid. The Holy Ghost had made them brave. They went from one country to another teaching and baptizing, just as Our Lord had commanded them.

"After baptizing the people, they also

confirmed them, so that the new Christians also were filled with the Holy Ghost.

"It was hard to be a Christian in those days," said Uncle John. "Christians were locked up in prison; they were beaten, burned, and even thrown to the wild animals. But the Holy Ghost gave them strength to bear their pains."

"I'm glad I didn't live then," said Ann.

"Yes," said Uncle John, "we do thank God we live in happier times. But even in these days, our souls are in danger of evil. That is why we need the strength of Confirmation."

"What does the bishop do when he confirms?" asked Tom.

"Well," said Uncle John, "first of all, he holds out his hands over those who are to

be confirmed, and prays that they may receive the Holy Ghost.

"Then the children come up to the altar
and kneel before him. The bishop dips his
thumb into holy oil and makes a cross on
the forehead of each one. While he is making the cross, he calls the child by his Confirmation name and says:

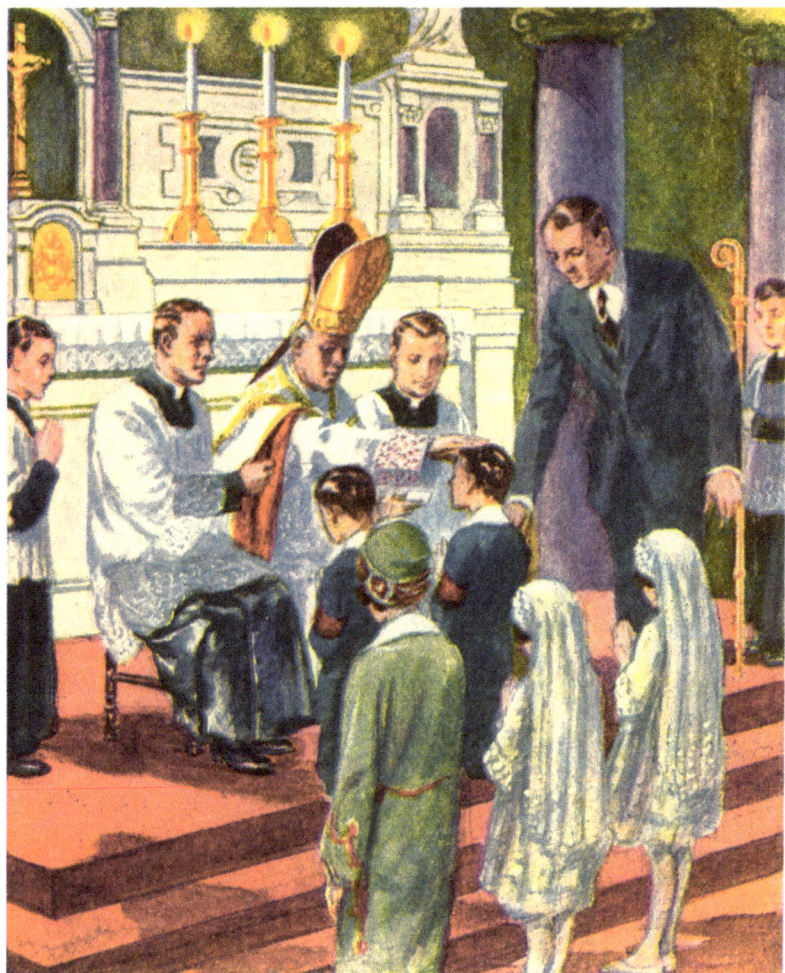

" 'I sign you with the sign of the cross,
and I confirm you with the chrism of

salvation, in the name of the Father, and of the Son and of the Holy Ghost.'

"At this moment, he lays his hand on the child's head, while the sponsor puts his right hand on the child's right shoulder.

"Then the bishop gives the child a slight blow on the cheek, to remind him that he must suffer everything, even death itself, for the sake of Christ.

"After that, the children return to their places. They are filled with the Holy Ghost. The bishop prays again, gives them his blessing, and the ceremony comes to an end."

"What did you say the bishop puts on our foreheads?" asked Tom.

"He puts chrism on your forehead, in the form of a cross," Uncle John replied. "Chrism is a holy oil mixed with a spice called balm. Of course, the oil is rubbed off before you leave the altar; but, remember, the Holy Ghost leaves a mark on the soul which will never come off. Even after you have died, it will stay there.

"How sad it would be for a Catholic to carry that mark of Confirmation to hell. It would make his shame and suffering even greater.

"But for a Catholic in heaven, that mark will be glorious. It will show that he has fought a good fight, and won his victory."

The church bell struck two o'clock. Uncle John, in surprise, looked at his watch. "You have heard enough of war and soldiers. Run along now," he smiled, "and let me have peace. Tomorrow we shall go out to see the soldiers' training camp."

"Thank you, Uncle John," cried the children, and away they went.

CHRISTIAN PARTNERS

(MATRIMONY)

"A letter for us," cried Tom, as he held up a little pink envelope.

"Whose name is on it?" asked his sister.

"Yours and mine. See for yourself," he said, handing her the letter.

They left the post office and crossed the road to the railroad station.

Tom opened the letter and read:

"Dear Tom and Ann:

"I have just written to your mother to tell her that Mr. White and I shall be married on the 8th of September. We want Tom to be the altar boy, and Ann to be our flower girl, at the wedding Mass. Mother

will let you come down a few days before, I hope, so that we may have a rehearsal."

News like this was too good to be kept a moment. The children rushed off to the farm.

"Aunt Margaret's going to be married," shouted Tom as soon as he opened the door.

"On September eighth," said Ann, in a voice almost as loud as her brother's.

"What's all this?" asked mother and Uncle John.

"I'm to be the altar boy," cried Tom.

"And I'm to be the flower girl," said Ann.

Mother took the letters from them, and read first the note in the little pink envelope. Then she passed it to her brother.

"Oh, no wonder you're so excited," she laughed. "Now I see what it is." And, sitting down, she read the long letter addressed to herself.

In a few moments, she spoke to Uncle John.

"Margaret wants to know how much notice she should give the priest."

"Tell her to visit the priest about a month before the wedding," answered Uncle John. "The young man should go with her and both should have their Certificates of Baptism.

"The priest will then make the arrangements for the marriage and, according to the law, he will read out their names in Church for three Sundays.

"May we go?" asked the children.

"Why, surely," mother answered. "I'll write and tell Aunt Margaret that you will be there."

"What is a wedding like, Mother?" asked Tom.

"Yes," said Ann, "tell us, so we shall know our part."

"Oh, your part is quite easy, Ann. You walk up the aisle just before the bride. When you reach the altar, you stand at the left side while the bride and bridegroom go up the steps to the priest.

"You will hear them say they take each
other for better, for worse; for richer, for

poorer; in sickness and in health, until death.

"Next, the priest blesses the bride's ring, the husband puts it on her finger, and, after some prayers are said by the priest, he begins Holy Mass."

"Am I right, Uncle John?" she asked.

"Yes, perfectly," he replied. "And, by the way, when the young couple declare they are ready to take each other for better or for worse, that is the outward sign of the sacrament of Matrimony. At that moment they receive a special grace from God."

"But what about my part?" asked Tom. "Is it hard?"

"No," his uncle replied; "you serve Mass as usual, but there are three times during Mass when the bride and bride-

groom go up to the altar steps. At those times, you hold the book for the priest."

"Why do they go up to the altar?" asked Ann.

"The priest says some prayers for them and the bride receives a special blessing. Then, of course, they go up to receive Holy Communion."

"Why don't they receive Holy Com-

munion at the altar rail?" Ann asked again.

"Because the Church wants to show honor to the young people who have just received the sacrament of Matrimony.

"At other times the proper place for the people is outside the altar rail, but on the happy day of their wedding, the Church brings them right up to the very place where Our Lord is."

"When I was married," said mother, "I was thinking of the Marriage Feast of Cana, as I knelt at the altar. You know what Our Lord did at that marriage feast, don't you?"

"Is it a story, Mother?" asked Tom.

"Yes, and a true story," she replied.

"Our Lord was invited to a wedding in the village of Cana. While He was at the feast, one of the waiters whispered that the wine was all gone. Just think how you would feel if there were not enough ice-cream at your party! That is how the young couple must have felt. They were poor and I suppose they had no way to get more wine.

"Our Blessed Lady saw the trouble. She asked Our Lord to aid the bride and groom. And He did. He told the waiters to fill up

some large jars with water. Then He changed the water into wine. This was His first miracle."

"Why were you thinking of that story when you went up to the altar?" Ann asked her mother.

"I was thinking of Our Lord making the young people in the story so very happy because He came to their wedding. And I felt happy because He was at our wedding. How near He seemed as we knelt there on the step of the altar! And how good He was to us! From Him we received all the blessings and graces that go with the sacrament of Matrimony."

"What are they, Mother?" Tom asked.

"They are helps from God," she answered—"wonderful helps which make a home happy.

"Catholic people marry in the presence of the priest. They know they are receiving a sacrament. They know, too, that the sacrament gives them grace. It gives them grace to love each other for God's sake. It gives them grace to be kind and patient and peaceful. And it helps them to bring up their children as good Catholics."

"Mother," said Tom, "the Dobbs boy from the city told me the other day that his mother used to be a Catholic. He was baptized, but his father won't let him be brought up as a Catholic."

"Did he say why?" asked mother.

"He said his father never believed in any religion. And, to avoid trouble at home, his mother will not let him go to church."

Tom's mother shook her head.

"Isn't that a shame!" she said. "How unhappy that woman must be. And what a pity to see the lad growing up like a heathen! But, it shows you why the Church wants Catholics to marry only Catholics. The Church knows that often there is unhappiness when the father and mother do not follow the same religion."

Just then an automobile was heard

coming up the road. Ann opened the screen door and looked out.

"Oh!" she cried, "they are lifting a boy out of the automobile."

Mother and the children hurried to the gate.

"Why, it's Jimmy Dobbs," Tom shouted. "What has happened, Jimmy?"

"Fell from a tree," he groaned.

Quickly they carried him into the house.

"Isn't it strange," mother said; "we were just talking about the boy!"

Soon the doctor came. He found the boy's right arm and collar bone broken.

"He must remain here," he ordered.

"We'll be glad to keep the little fellow," mother answered.

That night Jimmy's parents were excited to receive a telegram saying that their boy had been injured. They decided to go to him right away. On the way they passed a church.

"I'm going in to say a prayer," said Jimmy's mother. Her husband did not answer. He watched her as she went up to the altar to light a candle.

Did God answer her prayers? We shall see.

SICKNESS AND HEALTH
(EXTREME UNCTION)

When Mr. and Mrs. Dobbs arrived at the farm, Jimmy was a very sick boy.

"Pneumonia has set in," said the doctor. "The boy is in danger."

"Can't we send him to a hospital?" Mr. Dobbs asked.

"The trip would be too far and too dangerous for him," the doctor replied.

So it was arranged that Jimmy be left at the farmhouse, in the care of a nurse.

Uncle John asked Mr. and Mrs. Dobbs to go outside with him. For a long time they talked together.

When they came in, Uncle John went to the telephone and called the priest.

Then he said to mother: "The priest is coming. Let us get the sick-call set."

"I was praying that Mr. Dobbs would ask the priest to come," whispered Ann.

Meanwhile Uncle John spoke to Jimmy about Confession and Holy Communion. Also he told him what great help the sacrament of Extreme Unction gives to the sick.

Mother placed a small table in the room

WHAT YOU SHOULD HAVE ON A SICK-ROOM TABLE.

Cover table with clean white cloth. 1. Crucifix. 2. Two candlesticks with beeswax candles lighted. 3. Finger-bowl with water. 4. Glass of water. 5. Spoon. 6. Holy Water bottle and sprinkler. 7. Saucer with small balls of cotton. 8. Napkin. 9. Saucer with little pieces of bread and lemon.

and spread a white cloth over it. Then she put two candles on the table and between them a crucifix.

"Ann," said mother, "get the holy water bottle, a glass of water, a spoon and two napkins."

Ann got them and set them on the table.

Meantime, mother put on a saucer a slice of lemon, some small pieces of bread, and six little balls of cotton.

Everything was now ready.

Mr. Dobbs walked about, looking much worried.

"I hope your priest will help Jimmy," he said.

"I'm sure he will, Mr. Dobbs," replied Uncle John. "We Catholics have great faith in the priest and the sacraments. We believe that a person has a much better chance to be cured after receiving the sacrament of Extreme Unction."

"You will pardon me for asking," said Mr. Dobbs, "but what is this sacrament?"

Uncle John answered him in the words of the catechism. Speaking slowly, he said: "Extreme Unction is the sacrament which, through the anointing and prayer of the priest, gives health and strength to the soul, and sometimes to the body, when we are in danger of death from sickness.

"The priest prays for the person," he explained. "Then he takes blessed oil, dips his thumb into it, and makes the sign of the cross on the person's senses, that is, on the eyes, ears, nose, lips, and finally on the hands and feet.

"While he is anointing the person, he asks God to take away the sins that have been committed by those senses.

"One purpose of this sacrament is to restore health to the body, if it be God's will.

"Very often the sick person shows improvement at once. Doctors and nurses have noticed that."

"Yes," said Jimmy's nurse, "while I am not a Catholic, I must say I have known that to happen time and time again."

Mr. Dobbs excused himself and walked outside.

"I feel sorry for that man," said mother. "His life is so empty without God."

"Will Jimmy receive Holy Communion?" asked Tom.

"Yes, it will be his First Communion."

"But he is not fasting," said Ann. "He took some milk a little while ago."

"When anyone is in danger of death,"

answered her uncle, "he may receive Holy Communion even though food has been taken.

"When Holy Communion is given at such a time, it is called 'Viaticum,' or, as we say, 'our companion.' What a beautiful thought that is. Our Lord comes to us in Viaticum to be our companion on the journey to heaven."

"I hear an auto," said Tom. "The priest is here."

Uncle John lighted the candles on the table. One candle he handed to Tom. "You meet the priest at the door," he said, "and walk ahead of him to the sick room."

Everybody knelt as Father Smith entered the house.

Tom led the way to the sick room, as he had been told. Then he placed the candle

back on the candlestick. In a moment he came out and the door was closed.

The priest heard the little lad's confession. Then the door was opened and all went in to pray.

The children watched Father Smith give their little friend his First Holy Communion; tears were in their eyes as they asked God to cure him.

After that the priest took the holy oil and told Jimmy to close his eyes. He made a cross with the oil on each eye-lid.

With the cotton, he wiped the oil off. Then he anointed his ears, nose, lips and the palms of the hands.

Mother raised the bed-covering, and the priest anointed the soles of the feet. After this was done, he said some long prayers, first in Latin and then in English. Tom looked at Mr. Dobbs, who was kneeling at the bedside. He thought he could see the man's lips moving.

When all the prayers were finished, the priest washed his hands, first rubbing off the oil with the lemon and bread.

Before going, he spent some time talking to the family and the sick boy's parents. When he started for his car, Mr. Dobbs asked leave to ride with him to the village.

"I never saw my husband kneel down before," said Mrs. Dobbs. "A great change has come over him. If only little Jim gets well now, I'm sure our home will be ever so different."

"Well, Mrs. Dobbs," said Uncle John, "we are all praying for that."

Hardly was breakfast over next morning, when the doctor and Mr. Dobbs were at the door.

"Our patient has had a pretty good night," said the nurse smilingly. "What do you think of him, Doctor?"

"I'm very much pleased," said Dr. Ross. "If we can keep that fever down now, all will be well."

Days went by. Jimmy received Holy Communion each morning. Then came the glad news that the danger was over. At last the doctor said Jimmy might return home in a week or two. By this time Mrs. Dobbs was almost a member of the family, and her husband and Uncle John had become fast friends.

No longer was Mr. Dobbs an enemy of the Catholic Church. "I never understood your Church before," he told Uncle John; "and the trouble was, I did not want to understand it. But when my boy was dying, I saw things differently. That night, you people almost made me a Catholic."

"No one but God can make you a Catholic," smiled Uncle John. "But we shall pray for you."

"Good," replied Mr. Dobbs, "perhaps I'll surprise you."

As the auto drove off, Jimmy and his

parents shook their handkerchiefs as a last good-bye. Tom and Ann waved their hands until the car had passed out of sight.

"How happy they are now," said mother to Uncle John.

"Yes, they are," he agreed. "But I wonder how they would feel now if Mr. Dobbs had refused to let the boy receive Extreme Unction."

THE NEW APOSTLE

(HOLY ORDERS)

"Here is an interesting photograph," said Uncle John, as the family were looking at some picture. He had in his hand a picture of a small boy dressed in cassock and surplice.

"I was a little older than Tom," he said, "when that was taken."

"Did you think then you would be a priest?" asked Tom.

"Well, when that picture was taken, I did not," replied his uncle; but one day, I was at the funeral of a missionary priest, and I heard the preacher ask:

" 'Who will take the place of this good priest? Who will cross the seas to save poor pagans?'

"I felt like crying out 'I will.'

"The next time I went to confession, I asked the priest for advice."

"How old were you then, Uncle John?" asked Ann.

"About twelve, I think," he replied. "I remember, it was just before I was graduated from the parochial school. The priest told me to receive Holy Communion often and to wait until the term ended.

"Then he spoke to my mother and arranged for me to go away to study."

"And have you been studying ever since?" asked Tom.

Uncle John smiled at the lad.

"The time goes fast," he said. "I was in high school and college for six years, and then I went to the seminary for another six years."

"Twelve years altogether!" cried Ann, in surprise. "So you were studying to be a priest before we were born."

This thought made the children silent for a few moments. Finally Tom asked: "Is it pleasant in the seminary?"

"It is," answered Uncle John. "Just look at these pictures."

Tom looked at snapshots of the

building and grounds. Then he grinned.

"You can play ball there, can't you?" he said.

"Surely; there are baseball fields and tennis courts and fine places to play," said Uncle John. "You know, the students spend a great deal of time in prayer and study, but they must exercise their muscles as well as their minds.

"Here is another picture that will interest you," said Uncle John.

"It's a High Mass, with three priests," Tom declared.

"You're right, Tom," said his uncle. "It is a High Mass, but there is only one priest; he is standing at the altar. Behind him is a deacon; and behind the deacon you may see me."

Ann looked at the picture more closely.

"Yes, it is Uncle John," she cried. "Are you a deacon?"

"No. The bishop will make me a deacon when I go back to the seminary. I was only a sub-deacon when that picture was taken."

"What are deacons and sub-deacons?" Tom asked with real interest.

"They are men next in rank to the priests. It is their duty to assist the priest, and to serve God and the Church.

"Toward the end of his studies, a seminarian is made a sub-deacon. From that time on, he must read his office every day —that is—he must read certain prayers which require about one hour of his time."

Uncle John showed the children his breviary. "This is the book containing the office read by sub-deacons, deacons and priests."

Then he went on to say: "The deacon and the sub-deacon cannot celebrate Mass, but they do have an important part in the High Mass; also, at certain times, the deacon may preach and baptize and even give Holy Communion.

"In the very first days of the Church, the apostles found they needed helpers, so they chose seven holy men for this work and made them deacons. The first of these was St. Stephen.

"Enemies of Our Lord seized Stephen while he was preaching. They took him outside the city. Then these cruel people, while many looked on, threw stones at him until he was dead. Before he died, he begged God to forgive the men who were killing him.

"Now you know who the first deacon was," said Uncle John.

"Do you know who were the first priests?"

Tom answered at once: "The apostles were the first priests. Our Lord made them priests at the Last Supper."

"That's right," said Uncle John. "He made them priests and bishops too; and at that moment He instituted the sacrament of Holy Orders.

"This sacrament gives bishops, priests and deacons the power and grace to perform their sacred duties.

"Bishops receive more power than priests. They are like the apostles; they rule the Church in the name of Our Lord. And just as St. Peter was the head of the apostles, so the Pope is the head of the bishops. The Pope has the right to say who shall be made a bishop; and the bishop has the right to say who shall be made a priest."

"Supposing," said Ann, "that the bishop were sick on your ordination day. Could a priest ordain you?"

"No," said Uncle John. "There are two sacraments which a priest does not give, and they are Holy Orders and Confirmation. So, if the bishop were sick, another bishop would have to ordain."

Early in September, Uncle John returned to the seminary. Tom and Ann went with him to the station to say goodbye.

"You won't see me until my Ordination Day," said Uncle John. "Pray for me."

The children did; every day they said a special prayer for him. Then one morning in May there came an invitation to his Ordination and First Mass. Inside the envelope was a little note to Tom and Ann which read:

"Here are the front row seats I promised you."

*   *   *

The ordination was a beautiful sight.

Mother had read some books about the ordaining of priests and, the day before, she told Tom and Ann just what would be done.

The young deacons walked in procession with their bishop to the high altar of

the cathedral. All were vested in white,
and each one carried a lighted candle.

Tom and Ann recognized their uncle,
and kept their eyes on him during the long
ceremony. They watched him as he and
the others lay on the floor with their faces
downward, while the bishop and the priests
prayed for them.

They saw the bishop lay his hands on the head of each one to be ordained, and heard mother whisper: "Now he is a priest."

The young priests received the sacred

vestments. Their hands were blessed and anointed with holy oil.

Then the bishop held the chalice of wine and the bread to be used in Mass. Each new priest touched them. As he did so, the bishop said: "Receive power to offer the Sacrifice to God, and to celebrate Mass as well for the living as for the dead, in the name of the Lord."

The new priests knelt on the step of the altar and began to read Mass aloud with the bishop. The bell rang. Tom and Ann bowed their heads.

They knew that in a moment the bread and wine would be changed into the Body and Blood of Our Lord. They knew also that their uncle, who was now a priest, would say with the bishop the very words of Our Lord: "This is My Body. This is My Blood."

At last the sacred moment came; the bell rang again. As the bishop held up the Host, Tom and Ann said: "My Lord and my God."

After Holy Communion was over, the children saw the bishop again lay his hands upon the head of each priest while he said:

"Receive the Holy Ghost; whose sins you shall forgive, they are forgiven them.

Whose sins you shall retain, they are retained."

The ordination service came to an end. How happy Tom and Ann were! They had seen their uncle ordained a priest; he had offered Holy Mass with the bishop; and they had seen him receive the wonderful power to forgive sins.

While they were waiting to receive his blessing, Ann heard a familiar voice: "Hello, Ann."

"Jimmy Dobbs!" cried Ann.

"Hello, Jimmy; my, but I'm glad to see you here," said Tom.

The next moment Mr. and Mrs. Dobbs were shaking hands with everybody.

"What do you think?" said Mrs. Dobbs to mother. "My husband was baptized a Catholic yesterday, and he is going to receive his first Communion tomorrow at Father John's Mass."

"Yes; all year long I've been studying religion," said Mr. Dobbs, "and now I thank God I'm a Catholic."

It was a happy party which started back for the little village. On the way home, Father John spoke of Mr. Dobbs:

"Wasn't that good news on such a blessed day as this?" he said. "I've been praying for him ever since Jimmy was injured. During the year, Mr. Dobbs and I have written many letters to each other."

"When did he make up his mind to become a Catholic?" asked mother.

"Just about two months ago," said Father John. He went to a mission, and the grace of God touched his heart."

"Grace is a wonderful gift," said mother.

"Yes, indeed," Father John agreed. Then he turned to the children. "Do you remember the day when the airplane came down on our field?"

"Yes, I do," replied Tom.

"I spoke to you children that day about grace," said Father John.

"Yes," said Ann. "You told us it was a gift of God that gives us power."

"Good girl; you have a fine memory," her uncle answered. "But I told you, did I not, that we get grace in two ways?"

"Oh, yes," Ann made answer. "I know we get grace through prayer, and also through the sacraments."

"Ah," said Father John; "now you can understand about Mr. Dobbs. He needed the grace of God to make him a Catholic. And that night, when Jimmy was so sick, he showed he did believe in God, because he knelt down and prayed for the lad. God blessed him for that prayer, and now He has given him the grace to believe."

"Maybe God heard our prayers, too," said Ann. "We prayed for him every night."

"I'm sure you did help him through your prayers," Father John replied. "Children's prayers often work wonders."

* * *

Next day the village church was crowded. Ann and her parents were in the first pew with Uncle John's mother and father. Mr. and Mrs. Dobbs also had a place of honor.

Presently the church bell began to ring joyously. A few moments later the procession entered the church, which was beautifully decorated.

Tom walked first, carrying the cross. He was followed by the altar boys wear-

ing red cassocks. Then came the students from the seminary and the priests. Father John walked last, his fine gold vestments gleaming brightly in the sunshine.

What joy must have been felt by all present as they watched the young priest offer the holy sacrifice of the Mass! How their hearts must have burned with devotion when he changed the bread and wine into the Body and Blood of Our Lord!

And what a beautiful sight it was when the members of the family together with Mr. Dobbs, his wife and Jimmy all knelt at the altar rail and received Holy Communion from the hands of Father John!

Thus the first solemn Mass of Father John came to a close.

* * *

Not many weeks after, he began his journey to the land of the pagans. Today, perhaps, in some little chapel far, far away he will be teaching boys and girls about the grace of God and the seven wonderful sacraments. Let us add our prayers to those of Tom and Ann, that God may bless him and all the good missionaries in the world.

THE END

www.ingramcontent.com/pod-product-compliance
Lightning Source LLC
Chambersburg PA
CBHW050823090426
42738CB00020B/3461